UNDERSEA
LIFE
OF
AMERICA

UNDERSEA
LIFE
OF
AMERICA

To My Father

Irreverent, amusing and observant. No writer had a better mentor,
no anthropologist a better informant, no state a better governor,
no son a better father.

Acknowledgments

Many people have been unceasingly supportive in helping me
explore America's coasts and write this book. Ken Read and
George Buckley were companions on Pleasant Bay. Larry Madin,
Betsy Bang, Peter Tyack, Jim Hain and Sally Hacker lent books,
expertise and enthusiasm to the project. Ed Dow provided the all-
important last minute computer repairs.

The members of the Coastlines Project and the American Littoral
Society provided me with the time and opportunity to pursue the
goal. Gillian Lythgoe of Planet Earth Pictures provided
encouragement and pulled together this stunning assortment of
photographs. Trevor Hall my editor at Colour Library Books and
former cricketeer played longstop to my pitching.

My wife Kristina and daughter Chappell provided love, support,
comfort, and understanding during the general mania that ensued
as the deadline loomed.

CLB 2074
© 1990 Colour Library Books Ltd., Godalming, Surrey, England.
Color separations by Scantrans, Singapore.
Printed and bound in Italy by Fratelli Spada SpA
This 1990 edition published by Arch Cape Press, a division of dilithium Press, Ltd.,
Distributed by Crown Publishers, Inc.,
225 Park Avenue South, New York, New York 10003
ISBN 0 517 69509 X
h g f e d c b a

UNDERSEA LIFE OF AMERICA

WILLIAM F. SARGENT

ARCH CAPE PRESS

NORTH WITH THE SPRING

Caribbean Outpost; The Florida Keys

The East Coast of the United States spreads north with the beautiful clarity of a well-planned experiment. To the south are the tropical waters, coral reefs and mangroves of the Caribbean. A shifting realm of sand spans the middle coast from Florida to Cape Cod, and the rocky coast of Maine lies to the north.

Coral, sand and rocks; these are the three elements that define a coast anywhere on our globe. But on the East Coast they beckon the curious naturalist to explore and investigate.

The powerful force that tempers this coast is the mighty Gulf Stream; the blue god of the Atlantic that transports immense volumes of tropical waters northward. The waters hold much of their original heat, warming the western coast of Great Britain so that palm trees grow on the Scilly Isles and roses bloom at Christmas.

It is natural then, to explore America's East Coast by following the blue god north. The fairest time to travel north is in the spring, when a broad band of warming water proceeds inexorably up the coast. In its wake it brings hope, light, warmth and life.

The journey starts on the vernal equinox, the first day of spring. It begins on the Dry Tortugas Islands, the southernmost tip of the continental United States. This is Fort Jefferson National Monument. It lies sixty miles west of Key West, Florida.

Fort Jefferson rises from these tepid waters like a sepulchral mirage, a ghostly reminder of poor military planning. It was designed to be the Gibraltar of the Gulf of Mexico. Fifty-foot walls surround the entire sixteen acres of Garden Key. The fort was built to protect the entrance of the Mississippi River several hundred miles to the west. However, Fort Jefferson never fired a shot. During the Civil War it was held by Northern troops, but Confederate sailors simply had to sail around it, far out of cannon range.

However, Fort Jefferson did house prisoners, including Dr. Samuel A. Mudd, the physician who innocently set the broken leg of President Lincoln's assassin, John Wilkes Booth.

Though not very pleasant for prisoners, Fort Jefferson is a diver's delight. Clear blue tropical waters bathe the bountiful coral reefs and the seven small sandy islands that make up the Dry Tortugas.

These are the headwaters of the Gulf Stream. The South Equatorial Current meanders through the Caribbean sweeping up the seeds, spores and eggs of tropical plants and animals. Thousands of years ago it transported the larval ancestors of the coral polyps that built these reefs and islands. Now they thrive, the northernmost outpost of the Caribbean fauna.

Prowling the reef are yellowtails and angelfish. The water is filled with the noisy crunching of parrotfish as they use their fused, beak-like mouths to break off great clumps of coral. When frightened they defecate huge clouds of pure white coral sand. In a year they can convert bits of the reef into a ton of sand over every acre of the reef. The colorful fish are the transvestites of the reef, changing color and sex several times during their lifetimes. The brilliant greenish-blue fish is believed to be the terminal male.

A 300-pound grouper, seemingly the size of a human diver, swims close to the reef. Suddenly it stops and plunges toward a narrow crevice. Suction from his gaping mouth slurps in a struggling crab. It's enough to give a diver pause, as are the five-foot barracuda that arch their backs and gape their jaws when backed into a reef; an unmistakable sign of aggression that it is best to heed.

The low sandy islands that make up the Dry Tortugas are a birder's paradise. The artist and naturalist John James Audubon made a special trip to the Dry Tortugas to sketch the vast colonies of sooty and noddy terns. Today 120,000 sooty terns and several hundred noddy terns still nest on Bird Key Island.

A soft coral's branches form an orange tangle of life as it thrives beside the skeleton of a yellow sponge.

By dawn, the air is heavy with the pungent smell and raucous cries of thousands of territorial terns. By dusk, tropical sunsets silhouette aerial duels between wingswept frigate birds and boobies returning from a day of fishing. The duel usually ends when the harried booby regurgitates its catch and the frigate bird swoops down on seven-foot wings to snatch up the prize before it reaches the water.

Along the edge of these islands are quiet, shallow bays and lagoons. Brittle stars and lightning whelk hunt through miniature jungles of gently swaying turtle grass. Curious pulsating flowers lie on the bottom. When disturbed they turn over and swim away. They are actually jellyfish that harbor algae beneath their bell-shaped bodies. During the day the jellyfish swim to the bottom and turn over to allow the sun to nourish their abdominal gardens.

But suddenly the peacefulness of this quiet lagoon is broken. The dark form of a female shark looms out of the murky waters. She is being pursued by a slightly larger male. He streaks in from the side and bites her fin. The two roll over and about, roiling the shallow waters. Now there are other pairs going through the same violent dance. This is the rough and tumble mating ceremony of the nurse shark, a bit unnerving to behold only a few feet from one's naked legs.

But the most fantastic show of the reef occurs at night. It is then that the tiny polyps that make up the coral reef poke out of their calcareous homes to feed on passing plankton. Strange leggy basket starfish emerge from crevices to spread their finely branched arms toward the current. Flashes of greenish bioluminescent light signal the effectiveness of this deadly parabola. Tiny planktonic creatures swept into the waiting tangle of arms give off a final flash signaling their last moment of life.

But the surface of these nighttime waters holds the final and most magnificent light show of the night. For the past month the tail end of the Atlantic Palola worm has been developing into a new worm whose sole function is to swim to the surface and explode, releasing thousands of eggs and sperm.

It happens during the third quarter of the moon. Millions of worms back out of tiny fissures in the reef. The tail ends of their bodies start writhing and twisting in a circular motion until the worm breaks in two.

The tail has become an inch of frenzied bioluminescence. The glowing worm wriggles to the surface, where it starts swimming about in a feverish circle. It seems to give off more light the faster it swims, becoming a tiny whirling dervish of phosphorescent light. Speed, light and excitement mount. The sexual organs swell; then with one final burst, a bioluminescent explosion rips open the worm's body, scattering a blazing cloud of sperm and eggs.

By dawn all that is left are a few spent and empty worms swimming weakly on the surface and billions of tiny, wriggling larvae that drift slowly in the grip of the Florida Current. Some historians believe that the mysterious lights reported by Columbus on October 11, four hours before his historic landfall, were the mating ritual of these tropical "fireworms".

The Gulf of Mexico

It is the Florida Current that sweeps through the keys and veers north to power the Gulf Stream. Before joining the Gulf Stream, however, let's take a slight detour west, a pleasant loop into the sultry waters of the Gulf of Mexico.

Traveling up the west coast of Florida we encounter Cayo Costa, an uninhabited barrier island that protects the entrance to Charlotte Harbor. In the morning the beaches of Cayo Costa look like a newly plowed field. During the night herds of wild pigs root through the sand in search of shoreside mollusks and mole crabs.

Ephemeral spurs of sand arch into the Gulf of Mexico. They protect swaying acres of turtle grass beds where pipefish, conchs and seahorses prowl through miniature jungles.

But mangroves are the ribs of Cayo Costa. Red, white and black mangroves work together to colonize the shallow waters behind the island. A dense tangle of pneumatophores and prop roots binds together the sediments, creating new land where before there was only water. Schools of seatrout, sheepshead and snook swim through this protecting maze of roots in search of crabs and shrimp.

By dawn, flat-bottomed mullet boats skim over shallow turtle grass beds to encircle schools of the algae-eating fish. Porpoises pause in their play to roll over and scrutinize the occupants of the overhead boats.

A shrimp boat, returning from a night of fishing in the Gulf, streams through Boca Grande, its nets outstretched and drying like gossamer insect wings. In April this passage will be filled with hundreds of charter boats pursuing the widescaled tarpon that flourish in these waters.

North of Cayo Costa, mangroves give way to marsh grass as the Caribbean fauna yields to the cold. Only a day of freezing weather will defoliate mangrove trees, obliterating the shade that keeps the fast-growing marsh grass at bay. A shifting line separates the two ecosystems. During mild winters the mangroves push north. A single freezing spell and the marsh grass drives them south again.

Much of the north coast of the Gulf is disappearing. The remains of stilted beach houses on Alabama's Dauphin Island tell of storms and erosion. Louisiana is making heroic efforts to prevent the loss of land to the sea. But it is not so much to save the coast but to maintain the flow of tax revenue from offshore oil wells. Louisiana's waters extend three miles from the shore. Any loss of shoreline pushes the boundary back and robs Louisiana of revenue from licensing offshore oil wells.

The Gulf of Mexico has been subjected to the greatest influx of pollution of any marine area. The oil industry has been drilling out here since the 1940s. The Mississippi and a few lesser rivers carry eighty percent of the runoff of the United States into the northern Gulf of Mexico. The runoff includes industrial wastes from as far away as Minnesota. Pesticides and fertilizers come from as close as the cotton fields of Mississippi and as far away as the wheat fields of Kansas.

Hundreds of thousands of gallons of these wastes wash over the Mississippi Delta. There they pool up to form toxic reservoirs of pollutants that migrate along the northern rim of the Gulf. To a fish they must look like the towering clouds of the black blizzards, the raging dust storms that carried away tons of topsoil during the Dust Bowl era.

However, these underwater pools carry deadly toxins that poison fish and kill the animals that feed on them. Louisiana has almost lost her bald eagles, osprey and the brown pelican, her state bird, to these deadly pools of poison.

But offshore there are more beautiful scenes. Salt domes bulge from the bottom. They were formed when the Gulf of Mexico was almost landlocked and huge concentrations of salt were buried below sediments. As the salt heated under pressure it became plastic and pushed through the overlying sediments. Now these domes are favored places. Geologists seek them out for the oil that pools up around their deep underground cores. Some come close to the surface where flower garden banks harbor colorful collections of underwater plants and animals.

Brown, white and pink shrimp spawn around the base of these salt domes. Untold billions of their larval nauphlii drift from this shallow continental shelf toward the waiting estuaries of Texas and Louisiana. They join the blue crabs, oysters and fish that make the bayou waters of the Gulf a natural bouillabaisse of seafood delights.

As the shrimp hatch, they drift in the aptly named Loop Current that sweeps across the northern rim of the Gulf and rejoins the Florida Current flowing north through the Florida Straits. It has become the mighty Gulf Stream.

The East Coast

At Cape Canaveral, Florida, the waters surrounding the Gulf Stream change. Gone are the tropical fauna of the Caribbean, replaced by the south temperate species of the mid-Atlantic. They will be found north to Cape Hatteras, off the coast of the Carolinas.

But the Stream itself still carries tropical species. Long, gelatinous planktonic animals glide through a viscous world. Diaphanous blobs of protoplasm flash greenish orbs of annoyance when they are disturbed by passing creatures.

Windrows of sargassum weed harbor complex communities of crabs, fish and shrimp totally dependent on their tiny floating oases in the sea. The coral reefs and tropical animals of Bermuda thrive only because they are being constantly replenished by the Gulf Stream.

This is also the area of the East Coast's great migratory species. The Stream is replete with the big-eyed larvae of bluefin tuna. A female tuna has shed five million eggs into the stream and now these tiny motes of protein swim weakly with the current. Soon, however, they will become one of the ocean's strongest swimmers, weighing 1,500 pounds and migrating more than a million miles by their fifteenth year.

Bluefish also breed out here. One population spawns off northern Florida in early spring, another off of New England in July.

Cape Hatteras is the fulcrum for an invisible, leaky gate that separates the southern species of the East Coast from those of the north. During the winter the gate closes, forbidding the northward passage of migratory warm-water forms. But in summer the gate swings open and these species swim north to the next barrier, Cape Cod.

But Cape Hatteras is also the fulcrum where the Gulf Stream veers offshore. Turbulence from bottom topography creates swirls, eddies, and meanders. Inshore of the Gulf Stream, loops of Gulf Stream water sometimes encircle a core of colder water. This cold core ring meanders off on its own, sometimes maintaining its integrity for two years at a time.

During exploratory drilling in Baltimore Canyon and on Georges Bank, oil drillers used satellite imagery to see if any errant rings were sweeping their way. Like a violent underwater hurricane, these rings can destroy drillstrings and sweep entire populations of larval fish off shallow fishing grounds like Georges Bank.

But Cape Hatteras is also the fulcrum for a second gate, a gate that could hold the key to the severity of the consequences of the greenhouse effect. Eleven thousand years ago glaciers were retreating across the face of North America. When the flow of drainage water shifted from draining south down the Mississippi to draining northeast down the St. Lawrence, the resulting influx of cold fresh water pushed the Gulf Stream south so that it veered sharply to the east off Cape Hatteras rather than off Cape Cod.

The new flow of the Gulf Stream reversed the warming trend, plunging the world back into another miniature Ice Age. Many scientists fear that if the greenhouse effect alters the flow of the Gulf Stream it will greatly increase the severity of global warming.

North of Cape Hatteras are the beaches of Delaware Bay. Here occurs another unlikely confluence of migratory animals. It happens on the full moon high tide of May. Offshore, hundreds of thousands of female horseshoe crabs have migrated fifty miles across the continental shelf to reach these beaches at the peak of the full moon high tide. Each large female is replete with hundreds of tiny green eggs. Now they must navigate through a stagline of millions of eager male suitors.

As the tide advances, thousands of horseshoe crabs assemble on the beach. The dark forms of their shells are silhouetted against the lambent sheen of the moonlit sandflats. All that can be heard is the quiet scraping and scratching of their shells as they clamber over each other in their eagerness to mate.

A female digs a few inches into the moist sand just below the high tide mark. After resting, she starts to deposit her eggs. Hundreds are released before she drags her consort male over the spot so that he may fertilize the eggs. The rest of the males crowd around, eagerly competing to fertilize any egg the primary male might miss.

Within half an hour it is mostly over. All that remains is a small bolus of thousands of tiny green eggs.

The next morning the second part of this migratory drama unfolds. From as far away as the tip of Tierra del Fuego, the beaches of Brazil and the mudflats of Surinam, hundreds of millions of shorebirds have been winging their way north. Red knots, sandpipers, curlew and plover; all have timed their arrival at this beach to coincide precisely with the egg laying of the horseshoe crabs.

The eggs of the crabs are crucial to the birds' survival. In three weeks time they will have consumed over 300 tons of horseshoe crab eggs. Each bird will have doubled its weight in a few days of gluttony. The protein will enable them to fly nonstop for several days and nights to their breeding grounds 3,000 miles north on the Arctic tundra of Canada.

In fact, eighty percent of the world's red knots and sixty percent of the world's ruddy turnstones are concentrated on this single stretch of beach. But they will only remain for a few brief weeks while the crab eggs are most abundant.

It is only recently that scientists have discovered the importance of horseshoe crab eggs to the survival of these shorebirds. In 1989 an oil tanker ruptured, spilling thousands of gallons of oil into Delaware Bay. Had it occurred three months earlier people on three continents, thousands of miles away, would have missed the thrill of seeing hundreds of birds circle out of the evening sky to land and feed.

As long as horseshoe crabs continue to lay their eggs on Delaware Bay these shorebirds will add grace and color to beaches from Canada to the Caribbean and from Delaware to Brazil.

From Cape Hatteras north to Cape Cod numerous rivers and estuaries are the spawning grounds of the East Coast's anadromous species – fish, like salmon, that lay their eggs in fresh water, but live out their adult lives in salt water. The behavior reflects the recent glacial history of this coast.

It is thought that most anadromous fish were originally freshwater animals. As the glaciers melted back they swept many freshwater fish into the rich marine bays and estuaries. Here they could feed on vast stores of marine organisms.

But a few fish were able to readjust their physiology to allow them to return to freshwater ponds to spawn. The ponds provided their eggs protection from the numerous predators of the marine environment. Over time these fish evolved what scientists call a stable evolutionary strategy, permitting them to enjoy the benefits of both worlds; the protection of the freshwater ponds and the bounty of the saltwater ocean.

Today, the strategy that has worked so well for thousands of years is leading to a new problem. Striped bass, alewives, shad and herring have been in decline for the last twenty years. The reason is acid rain. During spring storms, pulses of acid rain enter the streams and tributaries where these anadromous species spawn. In a few short hours the increased acidity can kill all the fish eggs and larval fish living in the water.

Even if the fish survive, they face chronic pollution as they migrate up and down the East Coast of the United States, for many of these species, like the striped bass, never stray more than a mile offshore – offshore from one of the most developed coasts in the world.

By the first week in May the spring's warming has heated the waters south of Cape Cod. It is time for another great rite of fecundity.

Billions of foot-long Loligo squid congregate over patches of sand along the coast. At night the feeble rays of the moon filter through writhing multitudes of the succulent mollusks. Slightly larger males swim through the schools, trying to herd individual females from the pack. Some females are more in demand than others and the males must dart, grapple and bite their opponents in order to claim their prize.

When one male approaches another, a reddish brown spot pulsates between his eyes. Finally, one of the males glides below a female and attempts to grasp her around the middle. She pushes away his tentacles and darts to the side. Again he glides beneath her. This time she does not resist.

9

One long, thin mating tentacle gropes forward toward her fleshy mantle opening. Holding her with nine strong arms, he reaches into his own mantle and withdraws a bundle of spermatophores from his muscular penis. With one quick motion he plunges the bundle deep into her mantle, where he ejaculates tiny reservoirs of sperm.

After spawning the female swims to the bottom, where she finds a clump of fucus rockweed. She withdraws the sperm-impregnated egg capsule with her tentacles and proceeds to entwine it into the fronds with a series of twists and turns. The sight of the eggs elicits renewed frenzy among the other squid. One by one, other females attach their eggs until a pencil-long, gelatinous string of egg capsules sways in the gentle tidal currents.

Scientists, however, are generally more interested in squid nerves than squid sex. The squid's body is innervated with synchronized nerves that open and close chromatophores, specialized cells in the squid's skin that cause it to change color so rapidly.

But it is the squid's nerve-triggered escape mechanism that makes Loligo squid worthy of their own Nobel prize.

Squid are nervous, curious animals. They will approach a diver and stare into his mask with large, intelligent eyes. If the diver moves, the squid will instantly vanish. Actually it darts backwards quicker than the eye can register.

A nerve several times thicker than any in the human body triggers this response. A tiny electric spark coursing down the length of the nerve signals the mantle to contract, forcing a burst of water out of a siphon tucked below the squid's head. This sudden pulse of water propels the squid backwards, often leaving a confusing cloud of ink in its wake.

Much of what we know about how nerves operate comes from research on marine animals like horseshoe crabs, lobsters and squid; primitive animals whose ancient heritage makes them better than most land vertebrates for the study of many of life's basic mechanisms.

A ready supply of these valuable marine animals is the reason that scientists from all over the world perform their own annual migration to the seaside village of Woods Hole. There, at the Marine Biological Laboratory and the Woods Hole Oceanographic Institution, they tease apart nerves, peer into microscopes and collect samples. It is a small but significant part of mankind's ongoing quest to understand the mysteries of life on this planet.

Nestled into the elbow of that caprice of geology we call Cape Cod are the quiet waters of Pleasant Bay. For years it has been my own personal laboratory to study the role of sexual selection on evolution; today it also presents a natural experiment to study the possible consequences of sea level rise caused by the greenhouse effect.

On January 3, 1987, a vicious winter storm tore through Nauset, the barrier beach that protects the bay behind. Within a year, tidal currents had scoured a new inlet forty feet deep and a mile wide. For the first time in 140 years the full brunt of the Atlantic Ocean crashed into the shores of Chatham, Massachusetts.

Half a dozen homes were demolished or swept into the sea, twenty or thirty more are now teetering on the edge, and erosion plagues the entire breadth and length of the twelve-mile-long estuary. Today the tides in the bay are eight inches higher and lower than they were before the new inlet.

Overnight the town of Chatham has had to cope with the amount of sea level rise that most seaside communities will experience in the next thirty years. The town has not fared particularly well. Lawsuits, countersuits and rancor have torn the town's fragile social fabric. Close to a million dollars have been spent on sea walls, revetments and new channels that will only increase the amount of erosion.

But it is in the thousands of acres of swaying marsh grass that the real story may be told. Scientists believe that if the sea level rises more than half an inch per year, in three years it will kill the Spartina grasses that make up America's extensive marshes. If these marshes are destroyed, the United States will lose vital wetlands that are ten times more productive than the most fertile wheat field – wetlands that are also the nursery grounds for two thirds of the commercial fish species caught in the United States.

To date, the changes in Pleasant Bay have been subtle. A few cedar trees stand brown and withered at the marsh's edge, salt water has killed their shallow roots. Patches of *Spartina patens*, the salt marsh grass that makes up the upper marsh, have died, only to be replaced by more tolerant cord grass. Thriving new beds of light-dependent eelgrass show that Pleasant Bay is one of the few estuaries on the entire East Coast where water quality has actually improved in the past five years.

Perhaps new plants and animals will replace those killed by the rising waters, the marsh will expand and the bay will restabilize as a changed but equally productive area. If that happens the only losers will be the humans who built too close to the shore, humans who have lost the ability to adapt to the environment that has been changing ever since the evolution of life on earth three and a half billion years ago.

Around the tip of Cape Cod's Provincetown is a totally new regime. To the south of Cape Cod we were under the influence of the warm, blue waters of the Gulf Stream. Now we are in the sway of the cold, green Labrador Current. Tides that had been of little consequence from Florida to Cape Cod now take on greater meaning. Here they rise and fall ten to twelve feet on the highest tides of the month. In Maine they will rise and fall forty feet at the head of the Bay of Fundy.

But before heading toward the pristine waters of northern Maine, Boston Harbor gives us one more difficult lesson about man's impact on the oceans. Boston has the unenviable distinction of having America's most polluted harbor; dirtier than the harbors of Bangkok, Istanbul or Calcutta. Divers tell of swimming through a ghostly miasma of toilet paper that hangs just above the harbor floor.

Wildlife in the inner harbor is sparse, only a few highly opportunistic species can live in the polluted conditions. Over eighty percent of the adult winter flounder have cancer of the liver, lobsters are plagued with shell burns and food fish suffer from fin rot.

Below the surface, inrushing water sucks divers toward a twelve-foot-diameter outflow pipe. A grayish brown geyser of partially treated sewage boils toward the surface. A huge deflector prevents the wastewater from shooting into the air like a macabre welcoming fountain. Two of these outflow pipes pump half a million gallons of wastewater into the harbor every day. A massive brown slick of human waste stretches for as far as the eye can see.

But fortunately it is time to head further north. Gone are the sandy beaches and swaying marshes of the south. We are entering the rocky realm of Maine. The water temperature has plunged, making swimming a rapid and exhilarating experience. Curling green waves crash onto garnet-speckled rocks. The roar of the surf and the tangy smell of salt air suffuse this beautiful landscape.

Far up the coast, there is a shallow tidal pool hidden within a small cave that only emerges at the lowest of the year's low tides. It was to this modest cave that the great nature writer Rachel Carson clambered over slippery rocks It was here that she lay on a wet bed of sea moss to discover an elfin starfish suspended from the cave, one arm touching its own reflection in the pool. It was here that she came to revere the beauty of things that are ephemeral, things that exist only until the sea returns to reclaim its own.

And here, beside this pool, on the summer solstice, we end our journey north.

SOUTH WITH THE WHALES

Alaska

It is autumn. Our planet has swept through space, once again marking the seasons in its passage. We stand at the autumnal equinox, the first day of autumn.

This is Point Barrow, the northernmost tip of the United States. The northern lights, undulating curtains of shimmering hues, descend to the far horizon.

Overhead, all that can be heard is the quiet peeping of unseen birds as they traverse the nighttime sky. They will fly thousands of miles over land and ocean. They will use the stars and the earth's magnetic field to guide them to their southern destination. Some, like the arctic tern, will travel from the frozen tundra of Canada to the shore ice of Antarctica; the longest migration of any animal on earth.

Daylight reveals the true nature of Alaska's wilderness. Vast herds of Caribou migrate inland over well-worn paths. Tight pods of bowhead whales migrate close to shore. They are one of the last animals to leave before the fast-advancing pack ice. Built like ice breakers, the bowhead's magnificent arching skull can bash through foot-thick ice.

Onshore and off, these are the last surviving remnants of the Pleistocene era; the great age of mammals when vast herds of ungulates and powerful predators strode over every continent of the planet. Even surpassing the megafauna of Africa, these huge collections of Arctic mammals remind us of the world before it was overrun by our own species.

At Point Barrow the bowheads turn south. It was here that the world united briefly to save three gray whales entrapped in the rapidly freezing ice. Eskimos worked beside Soviet ice breakers to saw and smash the ice. For a few days they set aside harpoon bombs and ideology to save three animals in distress. Such cooperation is not uncommon in the frozen north where relatives often live almost in sight of each other on opposite sides of the US-Soviet border.

The bowheads must move quickly, for even their food is migrating downward. Dense clouds of amphipods and copepods are descending toward the ocean floor. They will remain 600 feet down until spring's abundance beckons them to the surface once again.

South of the Bering Straits herds of male walruses meet herds of females and their pups. Huge rafts of these compulsively gregarious animals lie back to belly on packs of floating ice. Always touching, these contact animals are so unlike their standoffish cousins, the seals, that bicker, bite and bellow when neighbors get too close.

Unseen, a polar bear watches the walruses from behind a pressure ridge of ice. Suddenly he crouches, springs and charges. Hundreds of two-ton animals clamber over each other in a wild panic to reach the safety of the sea. But one pup, trampled in the stampede, is too late to reach the ice's edge. In a single bound the bear is on him. He grabs a rear flipper and with a swipe of his powerful claw dispatches the unfortunate pup.

Carefully, the bear makes a neat incision around the dead pup's neck. He rolls back the skin, methodically consuming everything inside. In a few days all that will remain of the 800-pound infant will be an empty skin and a few well-picked bones.

Port Valdez and Prince William Sound resonate to the modern ear. Like Bhopal and Chernobyl, this was the site of one of the 20th century's worst industrial accidents. On March 23, 1989, the Exxon oil tanker *Valdez* ran aground on Bligh Reef, spilling ten million gallons of Alaskan crude into Prince William Sound.

The spill could not have happened at a worse time, or in a worse place. The spring overturn was occurring. Nutrients upwelling from the ocean floor were triggering vast blooms of phytoplankton, the drifting plants that form the foundation of the oceanic food chain.

Fish eggs and larval fish would soon be in the water, and the human economy of this area depends on those fish. Some fishermen make more than three quarters of their annual salary in just a few days of fishing for spawning herring. Spotter planes fly along this coast looking for huge white clouds of herring sperm that fill entire bays with their abundance.

At a precise hour the state radios a general alert that the herring season is open and a watery stampede ensues. Nets bulging with tons of gravid fish and egg-laden kelp almost capsize the boats. One year a boat made a single haul that netted the crew over a million dollars.

In as little as a few hours the state declares the season closed. Within days, egg-coated kelp and herring are being sold at the Tokyo fish market. Beside them are Alaskan King crab and salmon selling at over one hundred dollars a fish. All of these delicacies come from the Port Valdez area, described in 1967 by Dr. John Culliney as "the worst place in the United States to build an oil shipping terminal."

In addition to its valuable fisheries, Valdez harbors two natural hazards. Just to the west, a three-mile wall of ice towers over Prince William Sound. This is the Columbia Glacier and every year hundreds of blocks of ice cascade down its 300-foot face. Any one of these submerged icebergs floating down the sound could tear open the fragile hull of a supertanker.

Valdez was also the epicenter of one of the world's worst earthquakes, registering 8.6 on the Richter scale. The earthquake raised a ninety-foot tsunami, or tidal wave, that destroyed the town of Valdez. The quake affected half of the population of Alaska, crippling the state's economy. It uplifted a 100-square-mile area of earth's crust, the largest raised by any earthquake in history. Beachwalkers can still see a distinct white band of dead barnacles and tubeworms stranded ten meters above sea level by the devastating earthquake.

Prince William Sound will undoubtedly recover from the oilspill as it did from the earthquake before. However, it will take at least a decade for the environment to return to normal and for fishing to again become the lucrative livelihood it was before the spill.

SOUTH WITH THE CALIFORNIA CURRENT

The West Coast

The Aleutian Islands mark the beginning of the West Coast. It is from here that the California Current sweeps south, cooling and fertilizing the coasts of Washington, Oregon and California. Uninterrupted by capes and peninsulas, the current's influence creates a more uniform assemblage of plants and animals than found off the East Coast.

But the Aleutian Islands also mark the future end of the West Coast. The numerous volcanoes and earthquakes that dot this island arc give a clue to the immense forces that are at work below the earth's outer shell.

Just south of the Aleutian Islands, one giant plate of the earth's crust is plunging below another. The plunging Pacific plate carries most of the Pacific Ocean's sea floor and California's thin terrestrial rim west of the San Andreas Fault. One scientist has stated that in fifty million years the last refractory remains of Los Angeles, San Francisco and San Diego will disappear into the depths of the Aleutian trench.

It is these same majestically slow but inevitable forces that have created the spectacular landscape of the West Coast. Tens of millions of years ago, the tectonic plate that holds North America was moving west, riding over the Pacific plate. As the Pacific plate plunged below North America, it crumpled its leading edge, pushing up the West Coast's Sierra Nevada mountain range and pulling down its continental shelf to create the long, deep trench that contours the entire coast.

Few bays break the long sweep of the northwest's steep and rugged coast. The three-foot-tall dorsal fins of killer whales rise like scimitars from the waters of Puget Sound. However, far to the south the quiet waters of Oregon's Coos Bay provide some respite.

Shallow waters warmed by sunbaked mudflats slide over rippling eelgrass beds. Elk pause to graze in a nearby meadow while juvenile dungeness crabs scuttle along the leading edge of the incoming tide. This is the South Slough National Estuarine

Research Reserve, the first of seventeen reserves that ring the coastal borders of the United States.

Every year researchers and students come to the reserve to collect information that will help planners devise workable solutions to saving America's remaining coastal wetlands. So far there are seventeen other estuarine reserves that are well staffed and open to the public.

While the northwest coast is marked with some of the highest waves to hit the United States, the California coast is marked by instability and erosion. Deep canyons slice through the narrow continental shelf. La Jolla Canyon starts at the end of the Scripps Institute of Oceanography's pier, only 600 feet from the beach.

The West Coast's canyons pose problems for California beaches. Hundreds of small rivers and streams flow out of the nearby mountains carrying sand and sediment. Normally this sand would be picked up and carried south by longshore currents. However, canyons intercept this flow, creating giant turbidity currents that plunge down the canyons and deposit fans of sand in the deep ocean basins.

Once in the basins the sand is lost forever to the coast. Damming of the rivers and streams that provide this steady supply of coastal sand is starving California's famous beaches.

Anyone who has ever read John Steinbeck's *Cannery Row* carries their own mental image of Monterey, California. They know the field of dahlias where "the boys" – hobos from the dump – plotted innocent schemes to catch frogs and stray cats in order to cadge a few drinks from "Doc". "Doc" was the eccentric proprietor of Pacific Biological Laboratories Inc., "as strange an operation as ever outraged the corporate laws of California," according to Steinbeck.

The lab was an old house on Cannery Row, just down the street from Monterey's only house of ill repute. On many a night "the boys" from the dump, "the girls" from the house, the Nobel prize winner-to-be and the West Coast's pre-eminent intertidal marine biologist, "Doc" Ricketts, would carry on long philosophical discussions and boozy parties with people "of our own financial nonexistence."

There is a small coterie of marine biologists who cherish Steinbeck's lesser-known work, *The Log from the Sea of Cortez*. It was written when Steinbeck was embarking on a career as a natural history writer. It tells of the exploits of Steinbeck and his mentor, Ed Ricketts, when they rented a sardine boat to conduct a collecting expedition around the Baja Peninsula. Anyone who has ever hankered to be an old fashioned "bucket biologist" or wants to know the real John Steinbeck should read this wonderful book.

The demise of Monterey's Cannery Row would have made a compelling sequel to Steinbeck's *The Grapes of Wrath*. It was a tale of winds, currents, fishermen and sardines.

California sardines were the mainstay of Monterey's canneries. Their spawning is delicately tuned to coincide with the springtime blooming of phytoplankton. These blooms are made possible by upwelling zones created by prevailing winds crossing the California Current. Like a giant natural composting machine, the currents, winds and water work to fertilize innumerable acres of offshore water.

Soon this watery nursery is teeming with billions of sardine larvae feeding primarily on a single species of flagellate. However, there are also miniature monsters in these waters. A tiny carnivorous copepod, *Labidocera*, darts through the waters taking vicious bites of sardine flesh. For every sardine the copepods catch, five more are maimed and killed.

In the 1940s, the natural system broke down. Perhaps it was El Niño, a Pacific weather pattern that stifles the prevailing winds and shuts down the upwelling cells. El Niño and overfishing certainly were responsible for the rapid destruction of the Peruvian anchovy fishery that once supplied one-fifth of the world's catch of fish from a small patch of water off Peru and Equador. That catch plummeted from thirteen million metric tons to less than two million tons in three short years.

Today, the once colorful Cannery Row has taken on a yuppified, hip patina. The gleaming new Monterey Aquarium houses sharks, tide pools, and a spectacular 280-

foot kelp tank that dazzles its visitors. But the real thing lies just offshore.

A swaying jungle of 100-foot kelp fringes the rim of the Monterey Canyon, a yawning abyss that is the same size and shape as the Grand Canyon. From the shore it plunges 1,000 feet to the ocean floor.

On the surface, dozens of sea otters roll and play in thick fronds of kelp. Cormorants, gulls and pelicans paddle outside the bed, while a hundred yards offshore gray whales spout and cavort on the last leg of their migration south.

A mother otter wraps her baby in a few strands of kelp, takes a deep breath and plunges through the amber canopy. Bubbles ascend through the kelp that rise from 120 feet below. Golden shafts of light cut through the water, dancing and glittering on the fronds.

Finally the otter reaches the bottom, where sculpin-like cabezon and large-headed lizardfish watch her scuttling over the rocks. Sea anemones the size of dinner plates draw in their colorful tentacles and a fleshy sea hare, *Aplysia*, never pauses in her task of laying a delicate ring of sticky pink eggs.

The female otter scrambles over rocks and squeezes into a narrow crevice. Her back legs thrash through the water as she tries to reach the dark red tentacles of an abalone wedged deep between the rocks. Now she turns and wedges her hindquarters into the crevice. Perhaps she can reach the succulent morsel with her powerful hind claws.

Her efforts are to no avail. With lungs bursting for air she gives up, grasps a sea urchin with one paw, a medium-sized rock in the other and pushes for the surface.

Suddenly an ominous, dark silhouette looms through the fronds. But the frightened otter must continue her ascent. This time she is lucky. Instead of a white-tipped shark or eight-foot killer whale this is merely a playful harbor seal looping and gliding through the understory.

With a final kick the otter breaks the surface, looks about and swims toward her infant rocking gently in its kelpy cradle. After checking that her baby is safe, the mother rolls on her back and proceeds to break open the urchin with the rock tool she brought to the surface. Together the two otters feast, oblivious of the gray whales that are on the final leg of their long migration to the shallow breeding lagoons of the Baja Peninsula.

We have followed them from Point Barrow, Alaska, to San Diego, California, but now we must head west, our destination – the subtropical paradise of Hawaii.

Hawaii

Hawaii is an oasis, a luxuriant profusion of life flourishing in the deep blue desert of the Pacific Ocean. From the air, the islands stretch like a string of emeralds surrounded by silvery shards of beach and surf.

The peaks of each volcanic island is capped with a snow white crown of towering cumulus clouds. But the main island of Hawaii is merely the newest jewel in this necklace of tropical gems. Each was forged, one by one, in the seething cauldron of the earth's mantle.

Most people approach Hawaii by air, but to understand her origins, the best way to approach is by submarine.

Aboard the research submersible *Alvin*, it takes more than half an hour to descend to Loihi Seamount, twenty miles east of the main Hawaiian island. Some 3,000 feet below the surface, undulating curtains of silvery hot water spew from cracks and fissures. Towering chimneys of blackened lava jut from the ocean floor and the ominous rumble of the earth's interior can be heard through underwater hydrophones.

Below the submersible, an underwater volcano is pushing Loihi toward the surface. Perhaps in a hundred years, perhaps in a thousand, this seamount will explode above the Pacific. Molten lava will spew from its peak. Fire, steam and water will mix in an elemental crucible and the next Hawaiian island will be born.

It is a process that has continued for millions of years. A hot spot lies below the Pacific plate, the huge plate of the earth's crust that is drifting slowly toward the northwest. As the plate pauses in its passage over the spot, magma sears through the thin crust like a welder's torch burning through sheet metal. A seamount bulges toward the surface, its volcano erupts and a new island is born. Then, like a ponderous assembly line, the plate moves on, positioning a new piece of crust before Vulcan's torch.

This fiery birth is but the geological beginning of an island's life. Its biological development starts offshore, powered by a partnership between plants and animals, an intricate symbiosis that creates more living space than all of mankind's architecture. It is the teeming diversity of the coral reef, and it covers more of the globe than all of humankind's habitations.

The reef is the result of a living filter of coraline creatures that collect, magnify and recycle nutrients with unparalleled efficiency. The tiny organisms that make up the coral reef harbor zooanthellae algae in their tissues. The algae convert sunlight and carbon into organic matter by day, and the coral animals catch planktonic food by night. Together the two symbiotic organisms, a plant and an animal, use the few available resources, the sun and the few sparse nutrients, to produce a self-sufficient, recycling ecosystem unparalleled in its diversity and productivity.

The coral reef grows so fast it can easily keep up with the sinking of the new volcanic island. Soon a barrier reef rings the island and a lagoon of quiet water separates the reef from the island's sinking core. The end of this evolution occurs when the island has slipped below the surface and all that remains is a coral atoll marking the former perimeter of the old island.

The best way to explore this underwater oasis is to slip into the water on the reef flat along the island's edge. Below the surface, the black thrashing arms of brittle stars help clean bits of silt off the sponges, whose many pores offer the starfish nighttime protection.

Beyond the reef flat are the murky waters of the lagoon. There are only enough nutrients in the lagoon for a few patch reefs to grow in the 150 feet of murky water.

At the edge of the lagoon waves surge over the fringing reef. It is exhilarating but dangerous to ride storm waves over the reef's jagged crest. Below, myriad blue tang, angelfish and parrotfish flail in the current before securing safe haven in the reef's many crevices. The next wave finds them thrashing about once again, but somehow they never seem to be injured on the sharp coral. It is undoubtedly safer, but less exhilarating, for human divers to find a deep channel and swim out below the waves' surge.

The reef is a cacophony of sound. A constant chorus of snaps and pops create a background static. These are caused by thousands of pistol shrimp that have a specialized joint in their claw. The cracking of this supernumerary knuckle is believed to mark their territory and to advertise for mates.

Some of the reef is grooved with oval, white scars. These are the work of parrotfish similar to those in the Caribbean. Most of the organisms of the world's coral reefs share a similarity that stands in marked contrast to the striking differences found among land fauna on different continents. Most of these plants and animals evolved millions of years ago and have changed little since the geologically recent Isthmus of Panama blocked the free flow of larval coral reef animals between the Atlantic and the Pacific oceans.

Ahead, the hyperactive twists and turns of a tiny bluefish and yellowfish advertise that this is a cleaning station. Three-hundred-pound grouper wait in line and docilely open their huge mouths for the three-inch wrasse to dash inside to pick and clean bits of food from the grouper's teeth. A moment later the wrasse emerges from a gill slit and proceeds to the next customer.

Aggression and feeding are absent around these cleaning stations. Predator and prey line up beside one another to wait their turn. However, sometimes the non-aggression pact is broken, a three-inch blenny, whose movements and coloration exactly mimic those of the wrasse, dashes up to one of the waiting fish, tears a great chunk out of his flank and speeds away. The shocked victim is usually too slow to mete out retribution.

Not far away, a miasma of tiny fish swarm amongst the long, thin spines of a sea urchin. However, the urchin has strayed too far away from its daytime crevice. A triggerfish has spied it crawling across the sand. With a powerful jet of water, the triggerfish topples the urchin and tears into its unprotected abdomen.

But now it is time to venture beyond the buttressing reef. Swimming over the edge is like stepping into the Grand Canyon and descending in slow motion through a viscous blue fluid.

A deep, low, throbbing sensation pulses through the water. Gradually it gets closer. Now the empty blue vault is filled with whines and groans. Less than a mile away a humpback whale warbles nature's most complicated song. The whale has not eaten for several months and the song advertises his sexual desires.

Every winter male humpback whales pick up a song they sang a year before. They improvise, rearrange and add new verses to their scores, for scientists believe that only the most innovative and complex songs win the favor of the females. It is an elaborate sexual attractant, the underwater equivalent of the peacock's tail.

Now the singing is getting closer. Not far away a female humpback cruises with her calf. A large old bull escorts her closely, while several younger males jockey for position. But the female has heard this new, intriguing song.

One of the escorts rushes the advancing intruder. Their bodies clash and the bull's flukes rasp the singer's side. Now the old male swims up from below, pushing the intruder out of the water onto the old male's back. Eyes the size of grapefruit glower at each other. The old male carries fresh wounds around his flukes and blowhole, and his fifteen-foot pectoral fins are frayed from many a battle.

The singer is young and healthy. Agitation mounts. Now another of the males challenges the leader. He dives below the surface and blows a ninety-foot curtain of bubbles that hang in the water, "a line in the sand" challenging the intruder to cross.

But the female has made her choice. With a great gulp of air she dives deep into the shafting light. In darkness the two lovers meet. With long, gentle sweeps of his pectoral fins, the male caresses his lover's belly. Quivers run the length of her body as he sweeps over her genitals.

Now the two whales embrace. Long, white pectoral fins wrap clumsily about each other's bodies as they start a long, spiraling pirouette toward the surface. Fins flop and flukes flash. The excitement mounts. Gradually a six-foot-long penis emerges from its sheath.

Again the couple dives, spiraling down into the deepening blue. There, amidst the golden shafts of glistening light, the two leviathan's make love and a silvery burst of bubbles ascends toward the surface. Far overhead, the shrunken silhouettes of her two former suitors swim against the sun like tiny toys in a tub.

Soon the female will head back to the rich feeding grounds off Alaska. Her body will build up the fat and protein needed by her progeny and next winter she will return to regenerate her species in the warm, blue waters of Hawaii.

THE CARIBBEAN

A small garden of vase sponges feed on the microscopic plankton they filter through their feeding pores.

A pair of spotfin butterfly fish patrol their territory.

The graceful tentacles of an anemone and
the colorful pigments of a sponge are just
some of the beauties of a Caribbean coral
reef.

The baleful stare of a pair of mated lizardfish.

A banded coral shrimp sits amidst a soft
cushion of pink feeding tentacles.

Royal gramma fish swim over sponges and
the intricate branches of a soft gorgonian
coral.

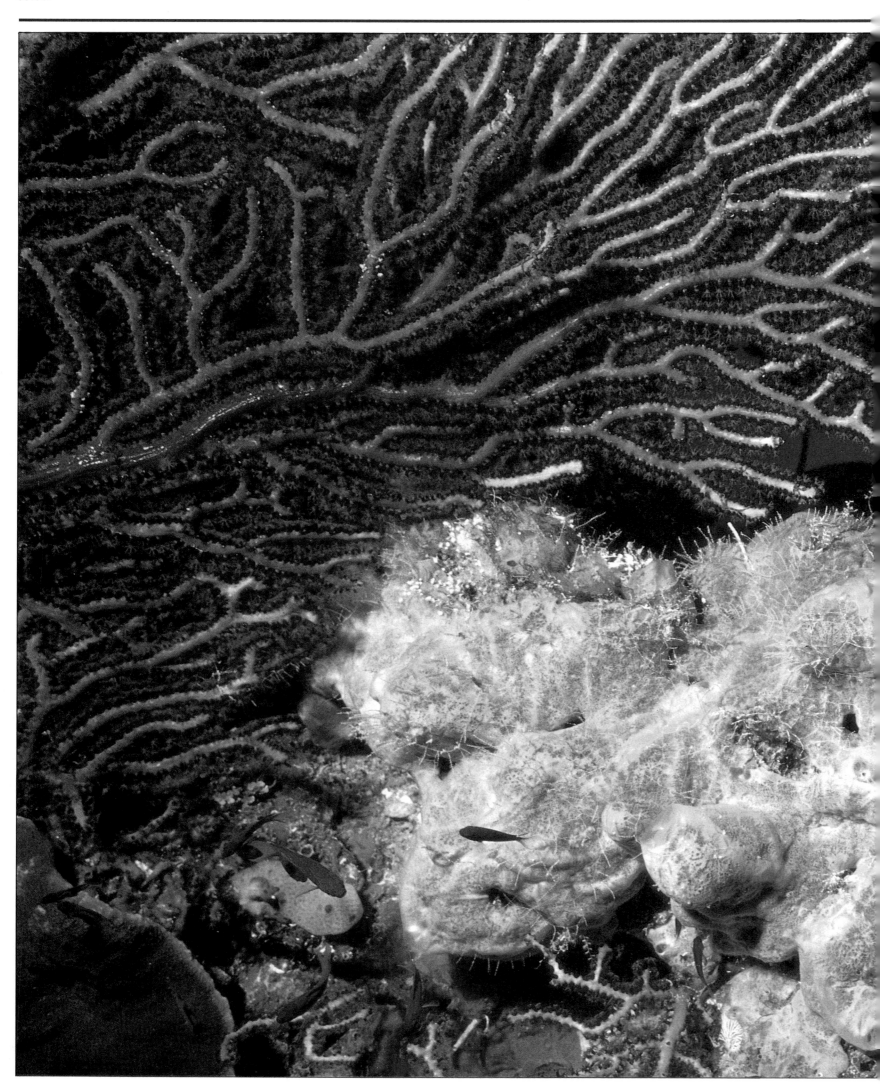

Facing page: a trumpet fish hangs upside down, mimicking a piece of coral. Any small fish that ventures too close will receive an unfortunate surprise. *Below*: the delicate gills of a fan worm comb the water for plankton.

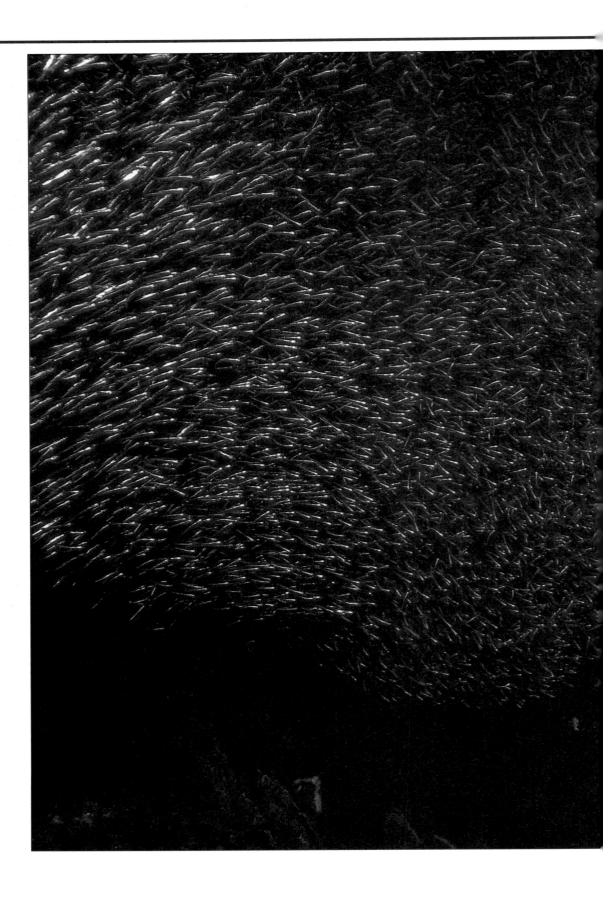

A swirling school of silversides sweeps past
a diver exploring one of the caves that
honeycomb a coral reef.

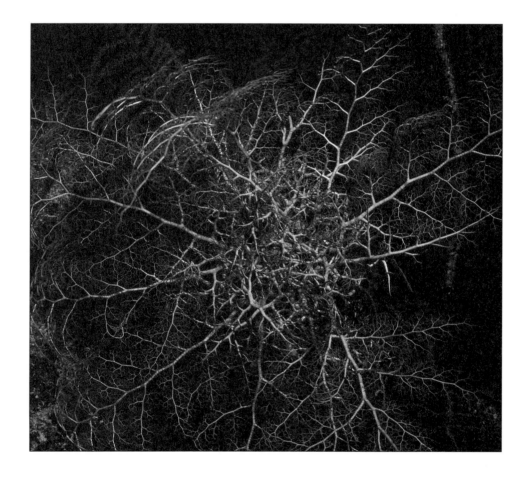

The soft, flexible branches of a sea plume contain hundreds of tiny feeding polyps. The branches grow at right angles to the prevailing currents that bring it its planktonic food.

At night, basket stars unfurl a deadly parabola of arms to capture luminescent plankton that sweep past in the underwater currents.

A hermit crab peers out at the world, its
eyes mounted on the tips of long eyestalks.

At night, the intricate patterns of the brain coral are covered by the delicate, stinging tentacles of the coral's feeding polyps.

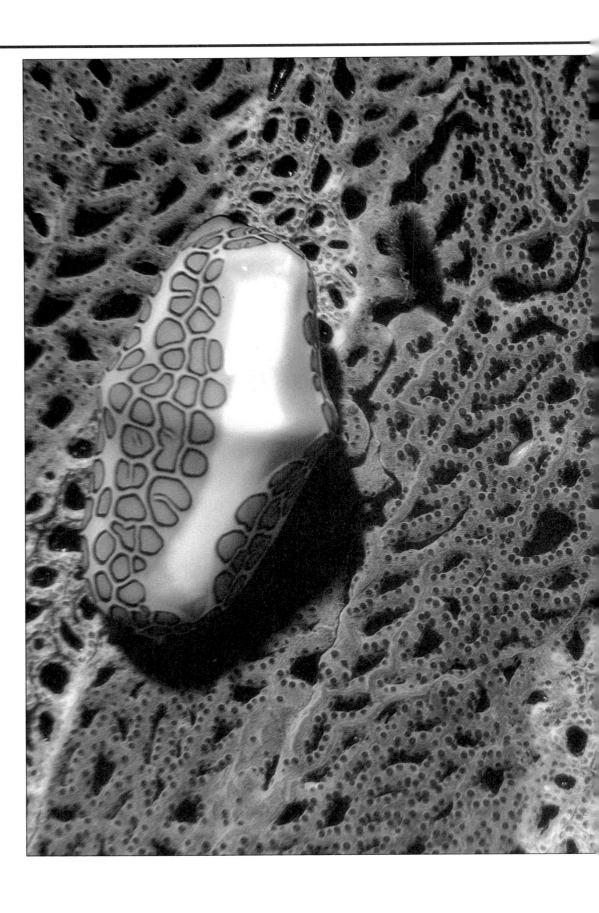

A pair of flamingo tongue mollusks leave a trail where they have grazed the living polyps off the skeleton of a sea fan.

A colony of sea squirts, or tunicates, thrive
on a coral branch.

Delicate sea fans provide a pastel backdrop
for the flamboyant pigments of a double-
barreled vase sponge.

The tentacles of an anemone can sting and
paralyze any small fish unfortunate enough
to blunder into them.

A spiny lobster emerges from its burrow.

The parrotfish goes through numerous color changes during its life. It feeds by breaking off large chunks of coral with its powerful, bird-like jaws.

A Nassau grouper sidles along the face of a
coral reef.

A tiger grouper poses before the tattered
backdrop of a sea fan.

Overleaf: feeding polyps of a gorgonian
coral emerge at night to capture passing
plankton.

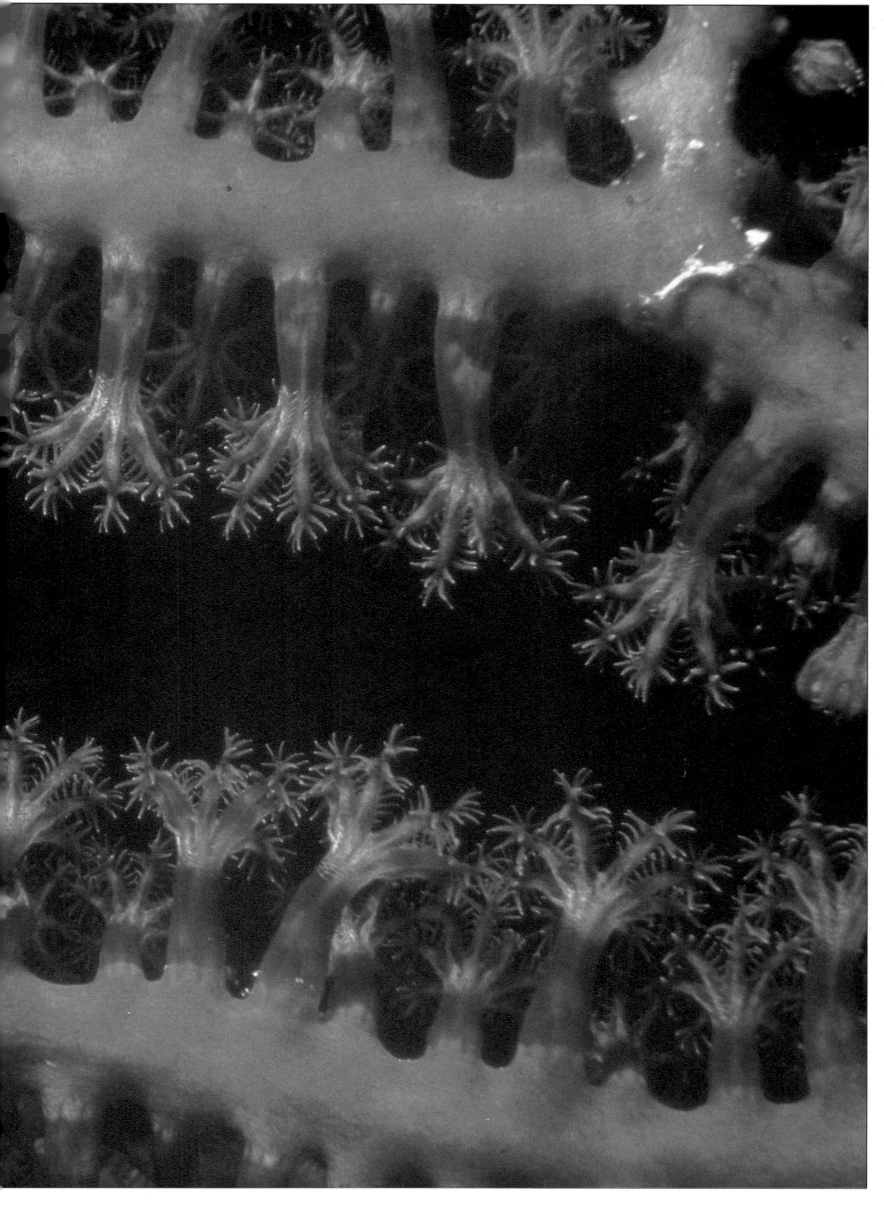

Facing page: a beautiful magenta vase
sponge clings to a coral wall.

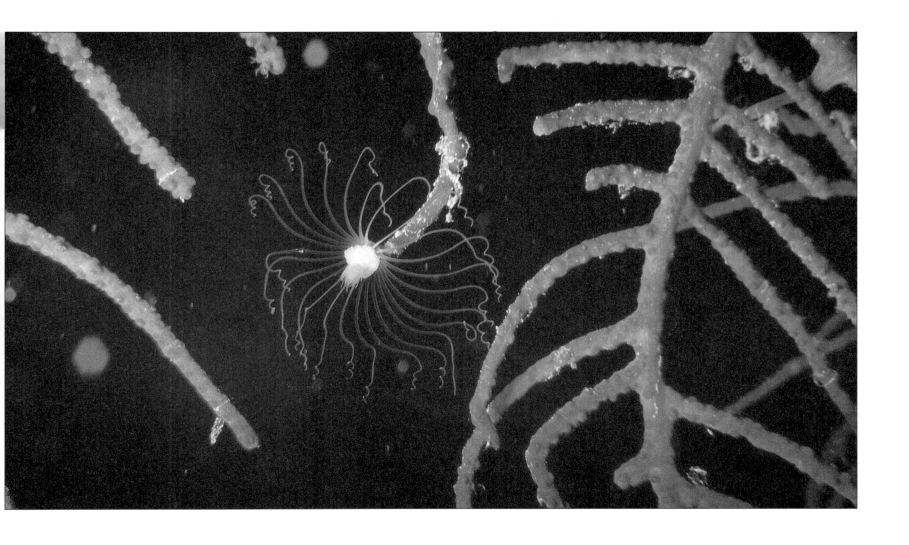

The stinging tentacles of a hydroid emerge
to feed.

A riot of grunts and snappers patrol the
structure of a sunken wreck.

The plumes of a feather duster worm
appear from a crevice in the intricate
designs of a brain coral.

A star coral emerges from its calcium
carbonate skeleton to feed.

The snaggle-toothed jaws of a moray eel
fail to faze an arrow crab feeding daintily
above the moray's burrow.

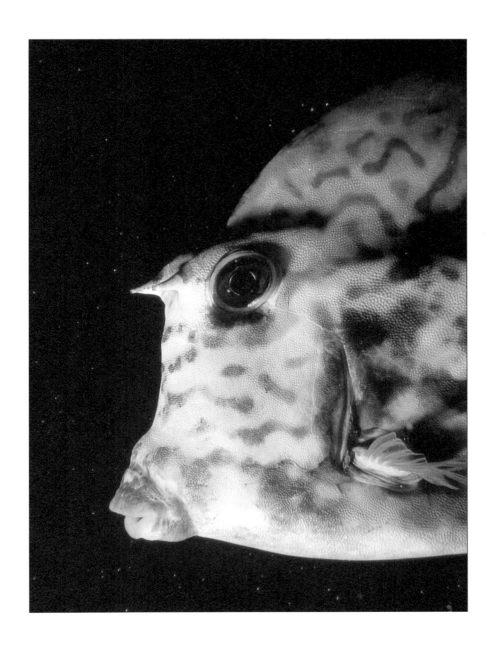

A hook and leader trailing from the mouth
of this four-foot-long barracuda provide
ample evidence of both its power and its
stoic nature.

A honeycomb cowfish puckers its lips to
crop tiny algae from the coral reef.

Facing page: the bright, clean lines of a yellowtail snapper stands in marked contrast to the pastel pinks of a vase sponge.

Above: with ruffled fringes, a nudibranch, or sea slug, glides gracefully across the reef at night. Top: a gray angel fish slides out of the darkness.

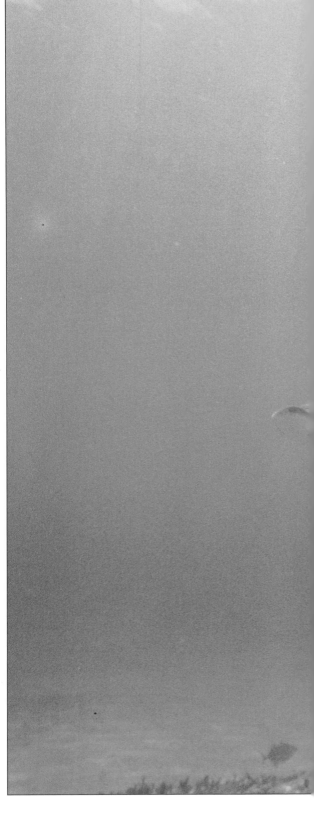

The fleshy body of a queen conch extends
out of its heavy shell to right itself.

Two remoras hitchhike on the belly of an
eagle ray.

THE GULF/ FLORIDA

Yellow snappers mob a diver for handouts.

The "upside down" jellyfish, Cassiopea, sits in the shallows where sunlight can reach the algae growing below its bell-shaped body.

A marauding sawfish – a sinister presence to the night gloom.

The deadly beauty of a Portuguese man-of-war, whose stinging tentacles can kill an unwary human swimmer.

The prop roots of red mangroves anchor
the fragile coast of southern Florida.

A commensal crab nestles into the
protective tentacles of an anemone.

A green nudibranch curls languidly over a
patch of algae.

Hunkering down, a well-armored calico
crab awaits lunch.

A manatee swims in the sun-dappled
waters of Florida's Crystal River. Formerly
land animals, these sea mammals consume
prodigious quantities of water hyacinths
and other aquatic vegetation.

A pair of bottlenose dolphin, possibly a
mother and calf, swim in close formation.

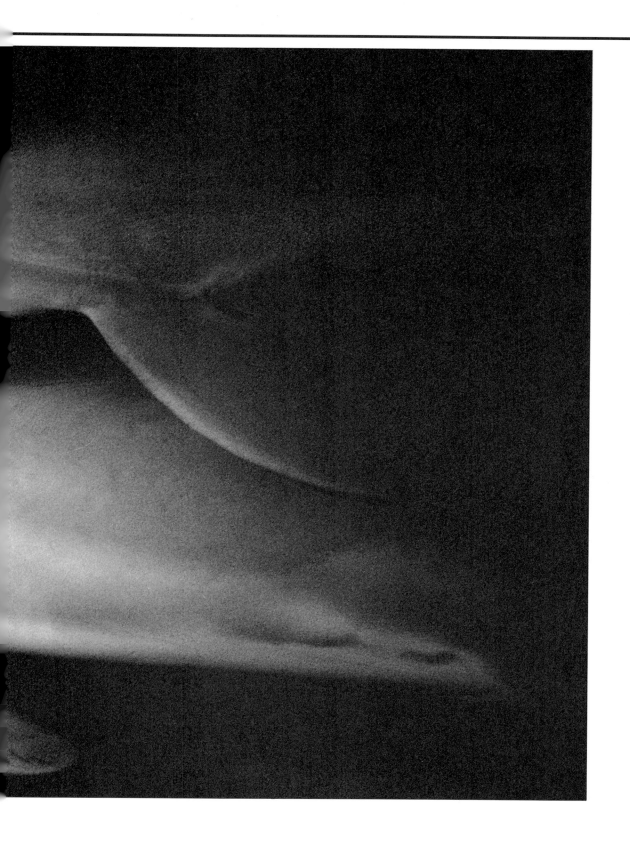

NORTH ATLANTIC

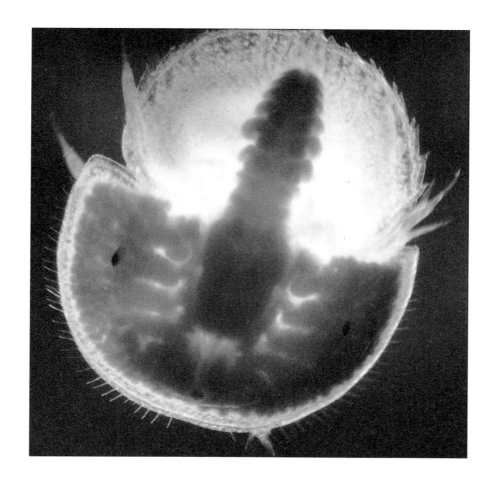

The lobster feast.

The newly hatched trilobite larva of a
horseshoe crab. Often called living fossils,
horseshoe crabs have remained unchanged
for 300 million years.

A pair of mating northern calico crabs.
The male's large claw protects the soft-
shelled female during mating, when she is
most vulnerable to attack.

Rows of color course down the length of a
squid as it surveys the diver. Squid are
large-eyed, intelligent mollusks that are
both inquisitive and nervous. Their body
colors indicate their feelings.

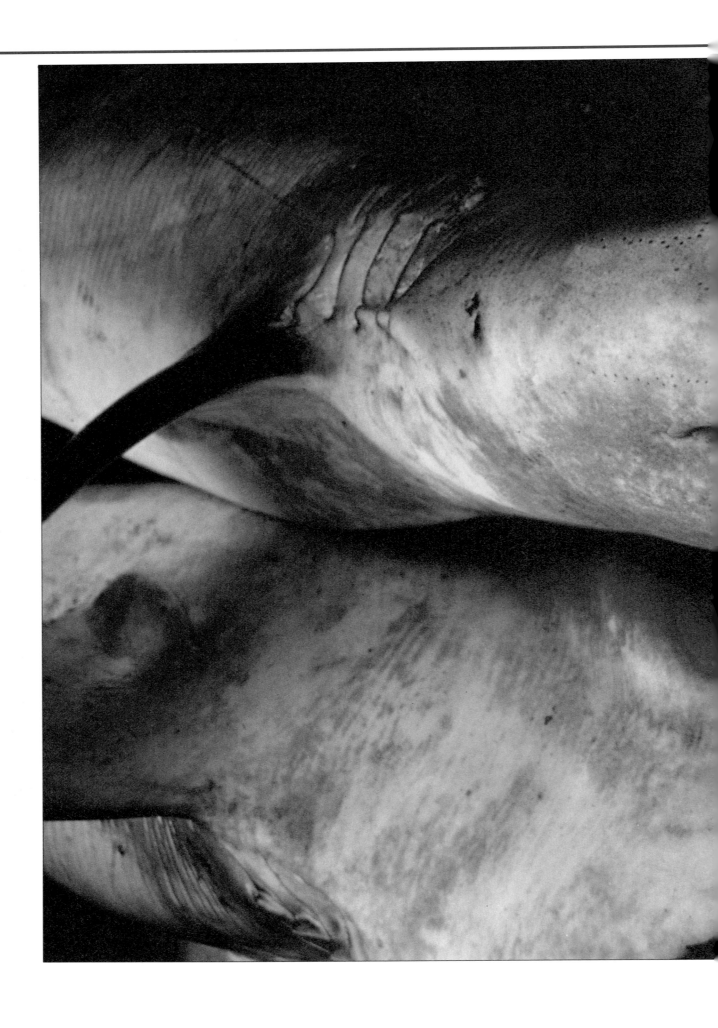

Even in the throes of a bloody death, this
blue shark continues feasting. Tiny rows of
dots around the shark's eye are the
ampullae of Lorenzini that allow it to
detect the electric field of its prey.

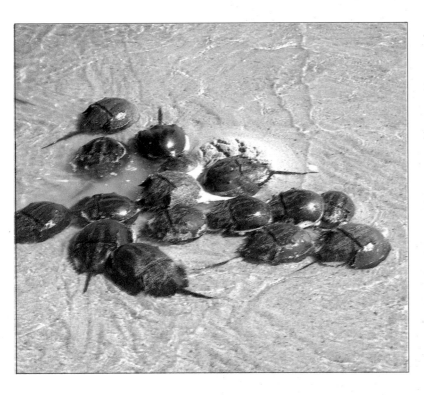

Lascivious male horseshoe crabs swirl
about a female crab burrowing into the
sand to lay its eggs.

A colony of Metridium anemones nestle
below an overhang encrusted with sulphur
sponges.

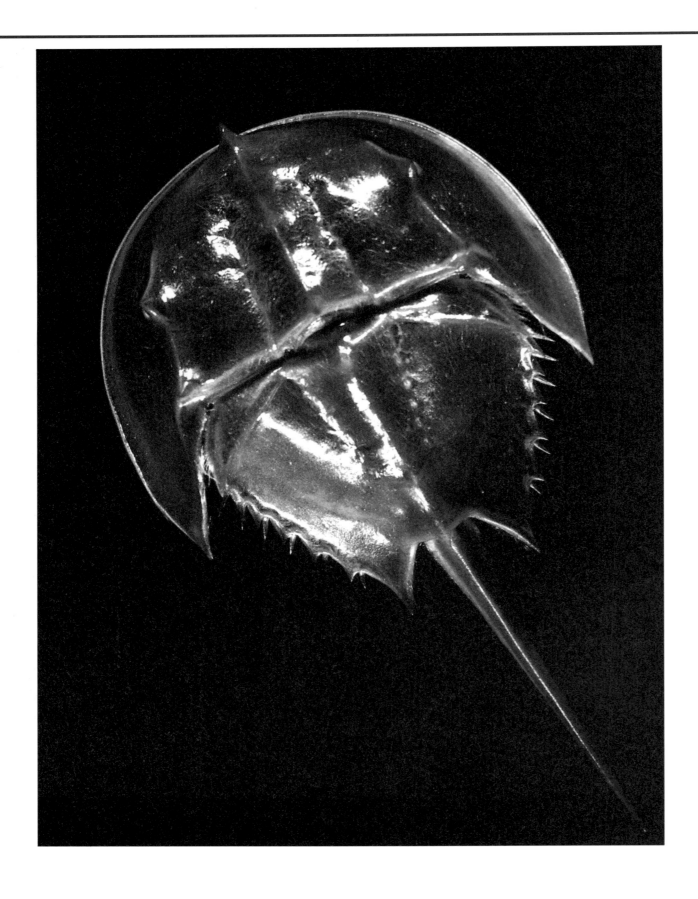

A horseshoe crab, shaped like the base of a
horse's hoof.

A wolf fish lurks beside a castoff bottle
encrusted with pink coraline algae.

A romantic evening on Delaware Bay,
where the setting sun casts a golden glow
on spawning horseshoe crabs.

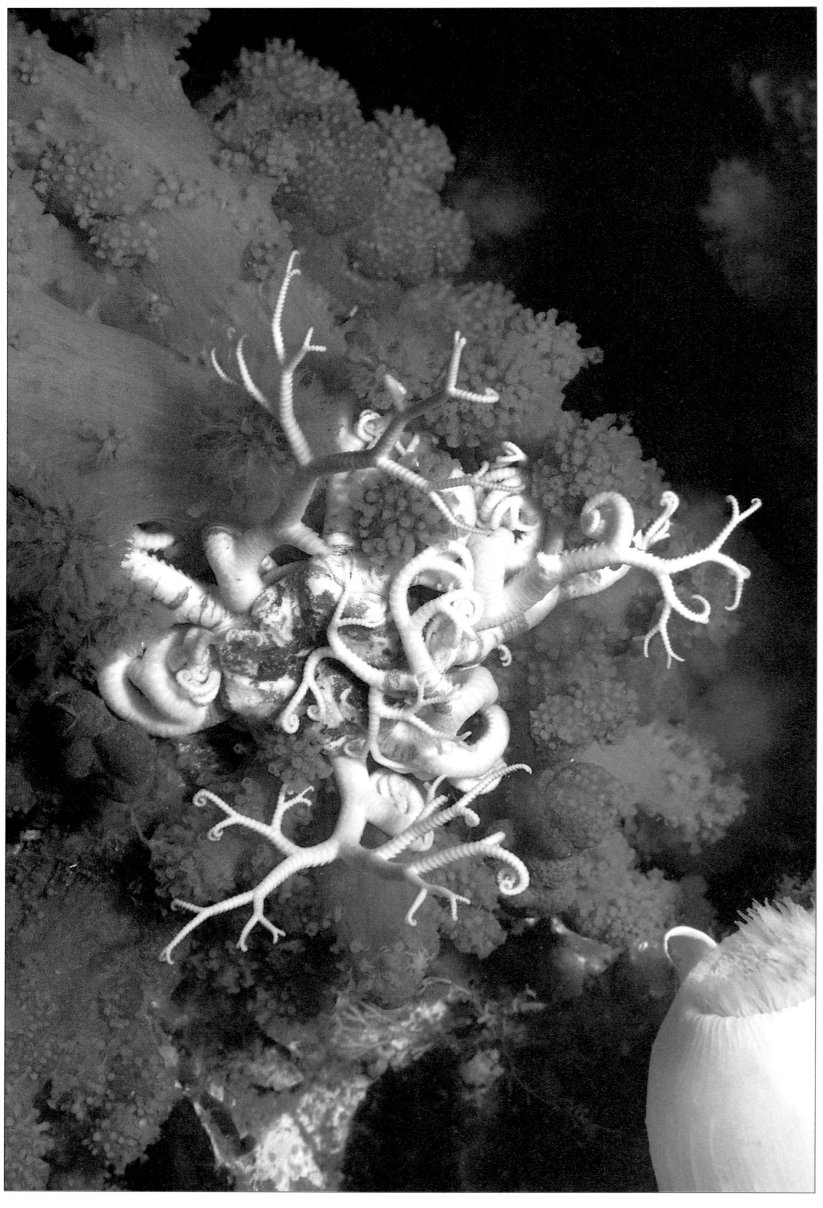

ALASKA

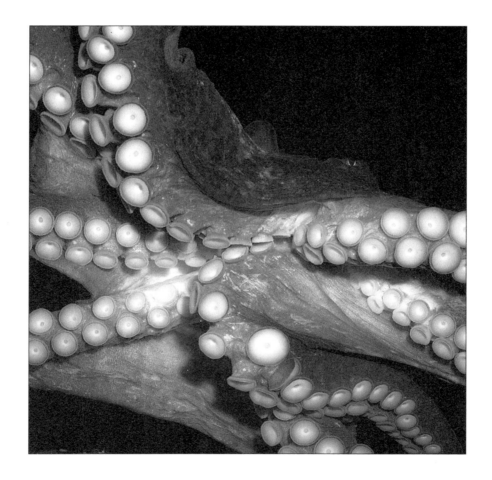

The tangled arms of a basket star emerge
from the scarlet polyps of a sea strawberry.

A threatening array of suckers on the
undersides of a giant Pacific octopus.

A school of Pacific salmon returning to
their natal river to spawn.

Northern fur seals cavorting amidst
swaying fronds of kelp.

A pack of prowling killer whales.

A red Irish lord sits on a coraline throne.

The tentacled heads of Metridium anemones sway in the grip of the Alaskan current like palm trees on an alien planet.

Humpback whales take the air in the
Seymour Canal of southeast Alaska.

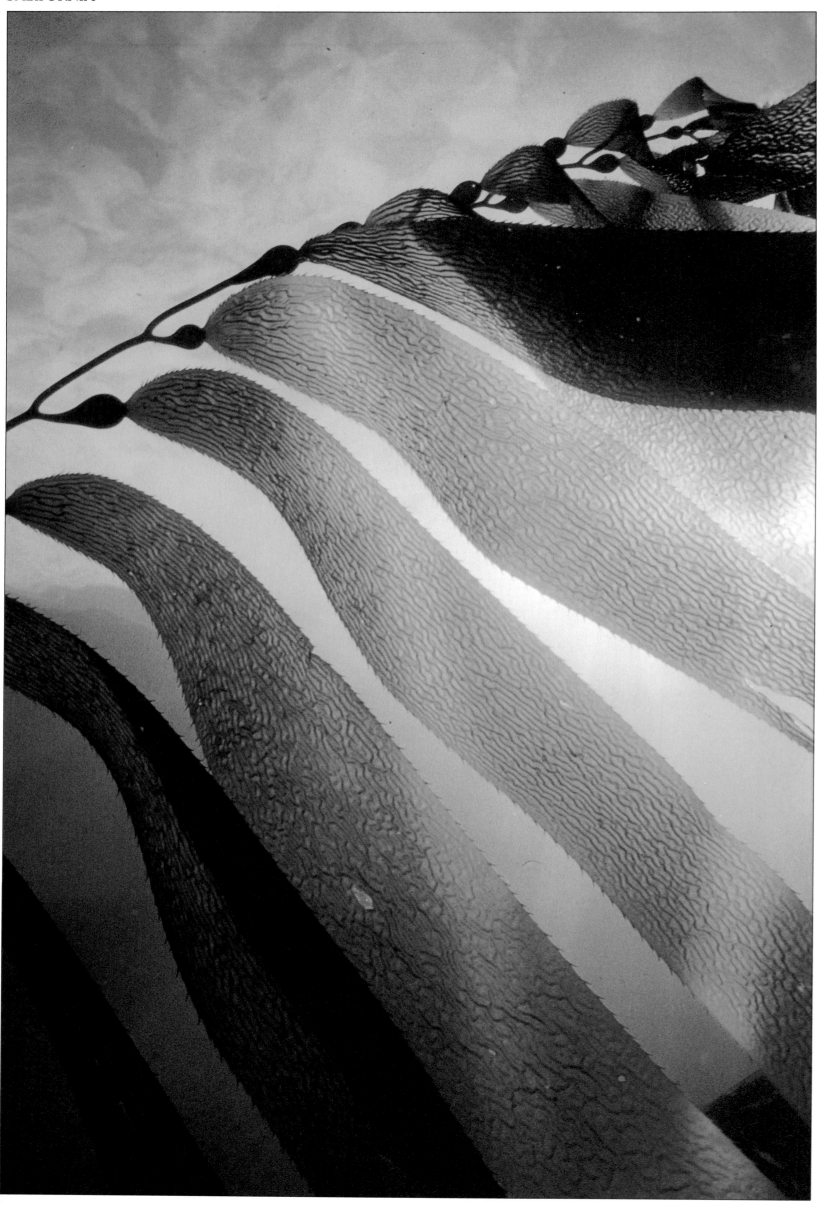

CALIFORNIA

Golden shards of light filter through fronds
of giant kelp.

A kelp crab – the "Darth Vader" of the
undersea world – waits for dinner.

Strawberry sea anemones in full plume.

A fringehead angler fish looks up
expectantly while dangling a deadly lure
above its waiting jaws.

Fronds of giant kelp float toward the surface, buoyed by gas-filled bladders called pneumatocysts.

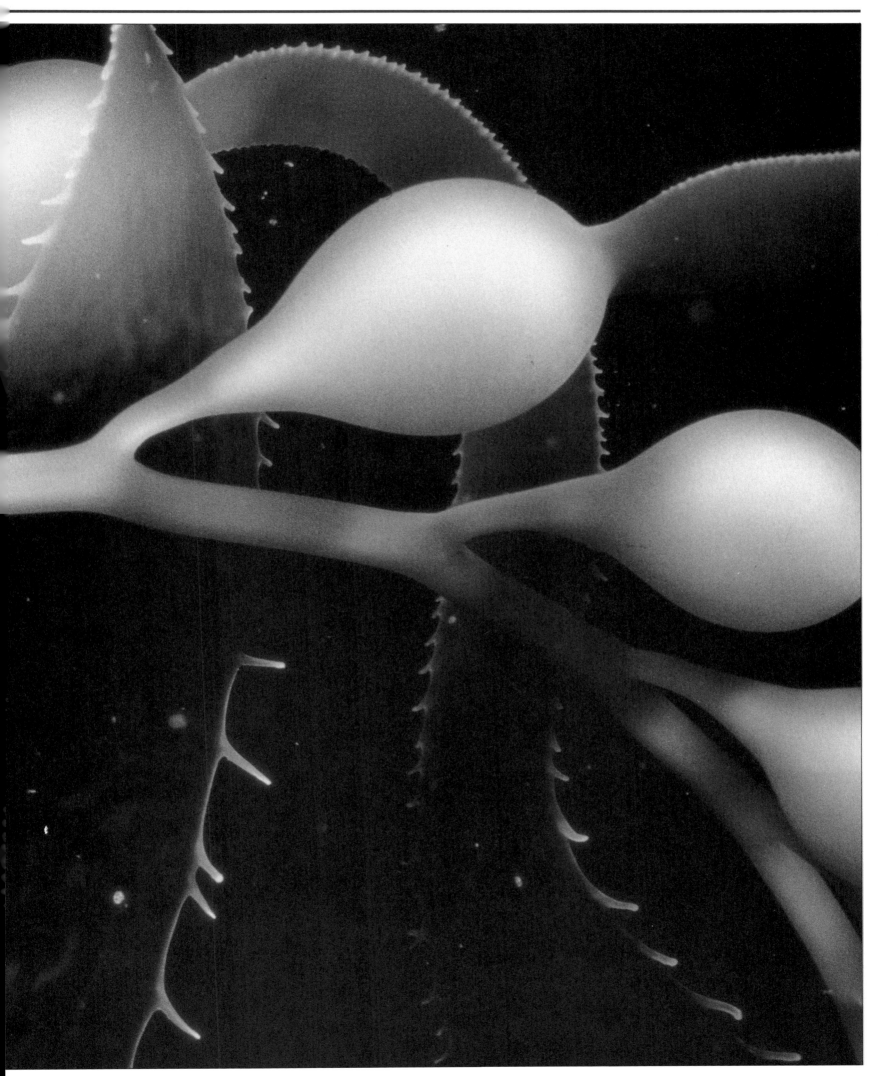

A California seal poses for the camera.

The Hermissenda nudibranch sports a
flashy coat of appendages, all armed with
stinging cells grazed from anemones.

A chiton clings to its favorite spot in the
waters off San Mateo, California.

Scrutiny by the malevolent eye of a horned
shark.

Overleaf: a California sea anemone extends its ruddy tentacles.

Mating squid turn crimson with excitement and lock arms. After mating, the female attaches its egg capsule to the tips of white egg cases already started by other females.

A twelve-pound lobster heads for an
uncertain future.

A flower garden of zooanthid anemones.

A pelagic jellyfish swims quietly over the billowing plumes of a sea anemone.

A flamboyant Garibaldi cruises over the
Californian seabed.

Eggs of a parasitic copepod stream from the
dorsal fin of a mako shark.

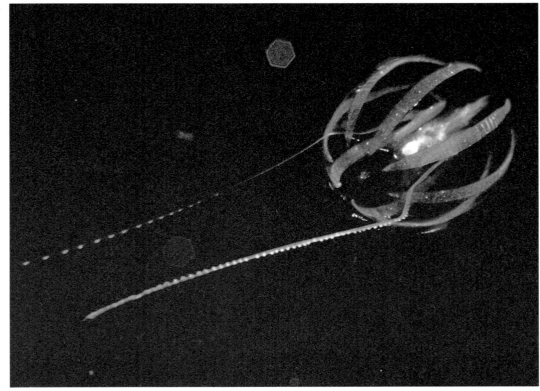

Iridescent light reflects off the rows of cilia
that a sea gooseberry uses to propel itself
through Californian waters.

A camouflaged turbot hides on the floor of
Monterey Bay.

The graceful silhouette of a blue shark looking for handouts from the bow of an overhead boat.

The close-order drill of a school of Northern anchovy. These fish have largely replaced the California sardine that supported Monterey's cannery row until the fishery collapsed in the 1940s.

The flowering plumes of the green anemone.

A pelagic jellyfish displays a tangle of tentacles and gonads that dwarf a diver.

A sea otter floats on its back in Monterey Bay.

A juvenile fish rests on the stipe of a kelp plant.

A ringed doris nudibranch sports a plume of gills as it crawls over the bottom of Monterey Bay.

A cabezon guarding its eggs.

Lice and barnacles compete for space on
the callosities of a gray whale.

A galaxy of multicolored bat stars.

Above: scarlet pigments camouflage a kelp fish nestled into the ruddy tentacles of a sea strawberry anemone. *Overleaf*: top shells near the seashore.

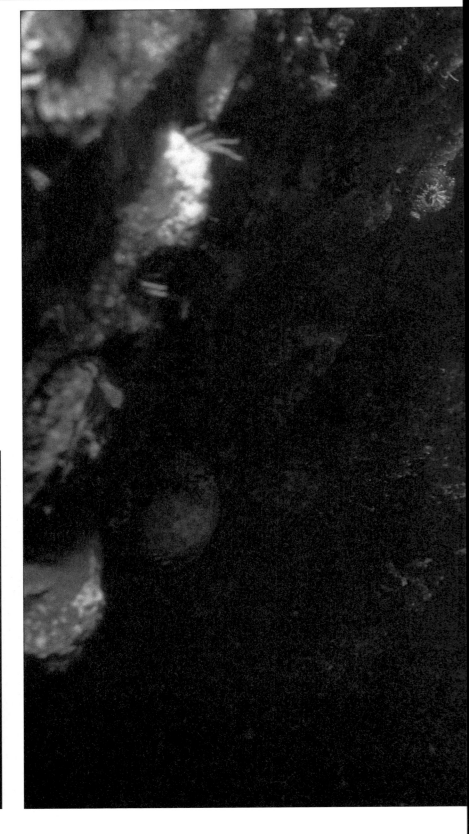

The gaping mouth and primitive backbone
of a solitary salp.

The fearsome jaws of a moray eel.

A rockfish flares its mouth and gills in an
unmistakable territorial display.

Gooseneck barnacles kick food into their mouths with rapid flicks of their specially modified feet.

The camouflaged sneer of a California
halibut.

With a simple mouth surrounded by
stinging tentacles, a fish-eating sea
anemone awaits its prey.

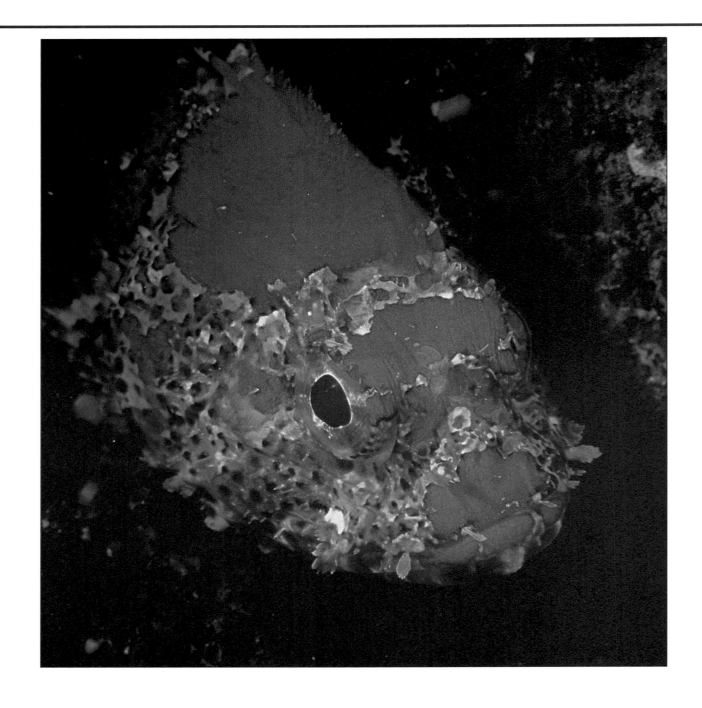

The frilled and gaudy face of a scorpion fish.

Purple sea urchins graze on kelp, their numbers held in check by sea otters, whose prey they are.

The pink camouflage of a snubnose sculpin
blends with a background of coraline algae.

A purple shore crab huddles into a rock
crevice.

Nudibranch eggs form a delicate filigree on
the Californian seabed.

Shards of light filter through a green
canopy of kelp as a lone diver prepares to
descend.

A purple sunflower star sprawls on the
bottom of Moss Beach, California.

The menacing face of a wolf eel.

HAWAII

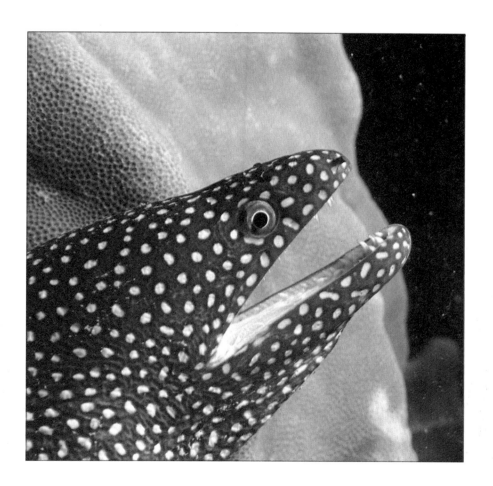

Flickering butterfly fish flit across the ocean floor.

A spotted moray eel keeps its mouth open to breathe.

The toothsome smile of lizard fish.

A ghost shrimp surveys its domain.

The Hawaiian islands grew from
underwater volcanoes and are still
expanding from lava flows that spill into
the Pacific Ocean.

Slate pencil sea urchins thrive on Hawaii's
coral reefs.

The scarlet face and generally ugly
physiognomy of a scorpion fish.

A manatee calf nurses from teats behind its mother's flippers, an arrangement which led sailors to mistake manatees for mermaids.

Big eye jacks patrol the clear, blue waters beyond Hawaii's coral reefs.

The feeding polyps of a Hawaiian hard
coral.

Tiny sensory hairs along a hermit crab's
legs allow it to pick up the chemical
signatures of food, mates and enemies.

A colorful Potter's angel glances back at
the photographer.

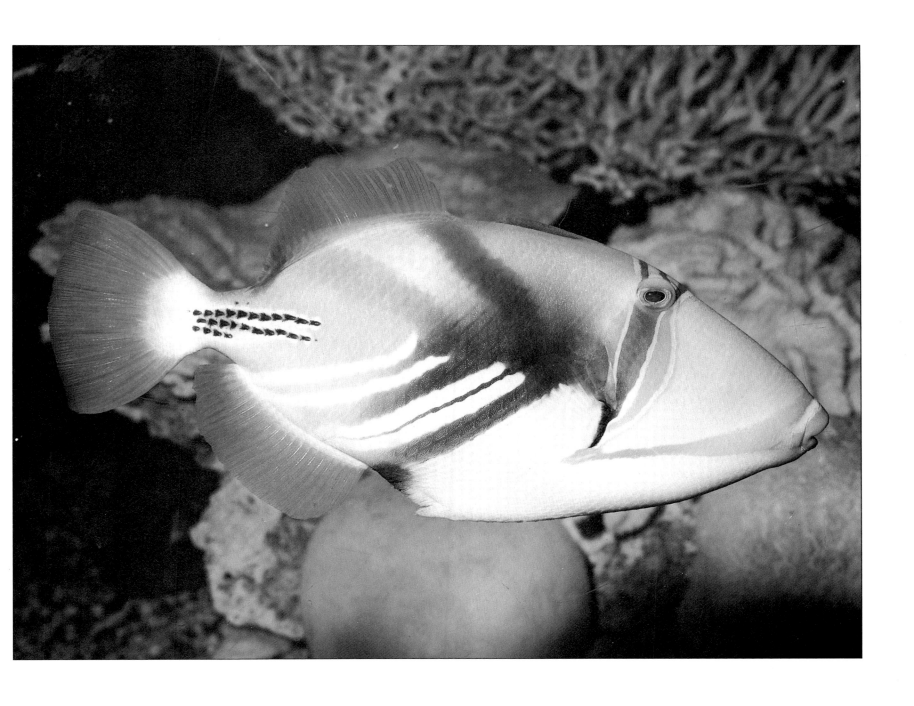

The huma huma nuku nuku a pauaa,
commonly called the Hawaiian triggerfish,
favors bold colors and abstract patterns.

A crab sits amongst a colorful tapestry of
anemones and coraline algae.

A breaching humpback whale waves over
its shoulder as it executes a perfect
backflip.

The baleful stare of a green sea turtle.

Overleaf: under magnification, a parrotfish's eye looks like an abstract watercolor.

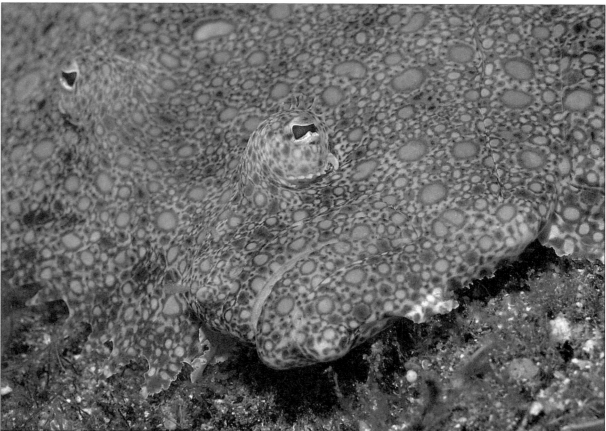

Above: the cockeyed appearance of a camouflaged peacock flounder.

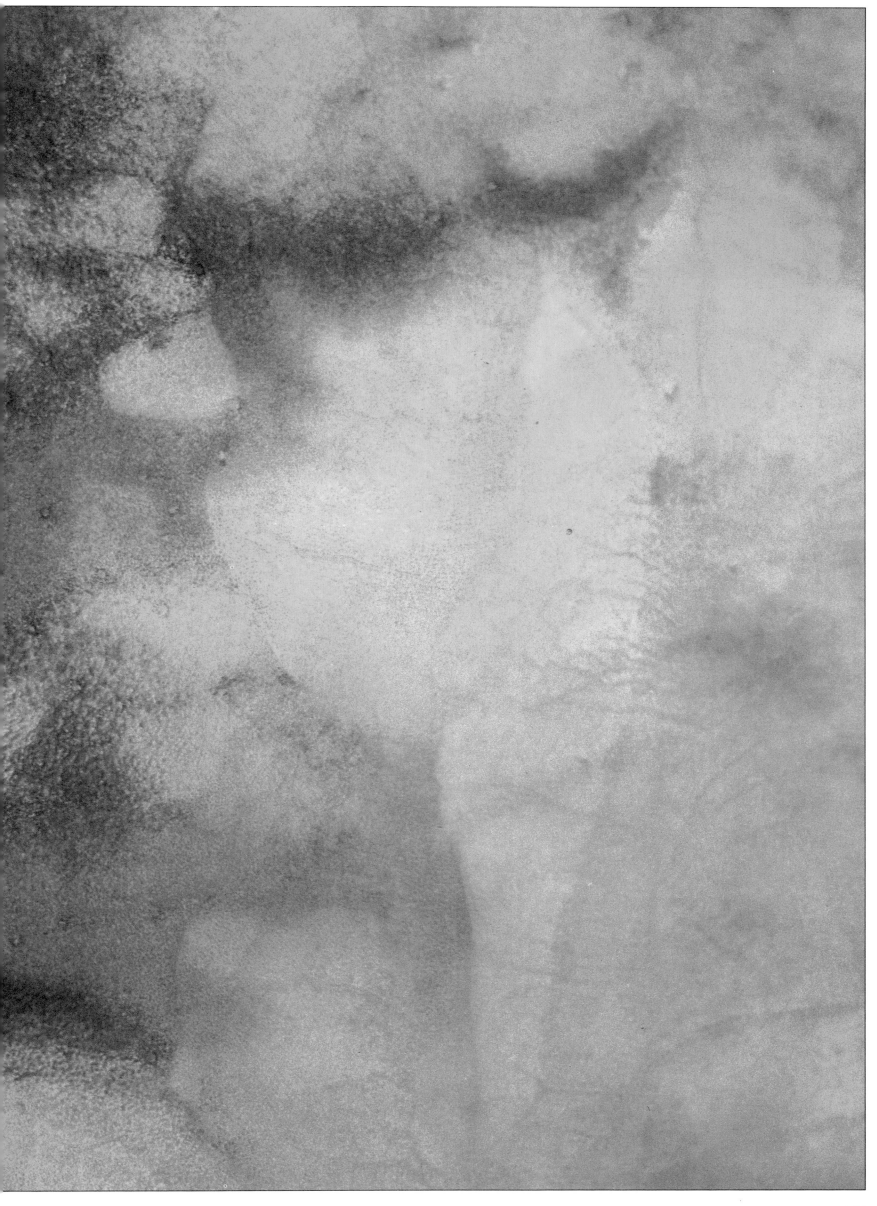